Helping a Friend Walk Through Grief

I0101854

Lee Joyner

ISBN-10:0986110205
ISBN-13:9780986110207

CONTENTS

ACKNOWLEDGMENTS

A book is never written by only one person. Every book, this one included, had a number of people who worked on it. I cannot begin to thank everyone who had a part in writing this book. They would include various hospice workers, pastors and bereaved who have given me feedback on good and bad responses. I have used all of this input in writing this book. I do want to say thank you to Judy Clark, Lisa Thomas and Jan White for their help in editing. Thank you to the class at Southside Baptist Church, Andalusia, AL. You helped solidify several of the ideas that were used in this book.

1 UNDERSTANDING GRIEF

If you want to help someone who is dealing with grief, the first thing to do is try to understand something about grief. I cannot turn you into a counselor. That is not the purpose of this book. I am not going to give you all the answers; no one has all the answers. While you will not become an expert in grief after reading this book, if you are going to help someone through their grief you need to understand something about grief.

In American society, which is the only one I know very much about, we are not equipped to deal with grief. Rather than deal with it, we prefer to ignore it. Most companies only give a person a week off, or maybe two, at the most, for bereavement. Afterward, that person is expected to be back at work and functioning at one hundred percent. Psychologists tell us this is not reasonable for most people, yet we continue to expect it. When an individual comes in contact with a person expressing grief, the first thing they do is try to get them to stop. We try to stop the tears of one who is crying over a loss, yet those tears are just what is needed to help that person overcome the grief. We try to stop the tears because we are uncomfortable. This is more about our comfort than helping the person who is in grief.

The way we are conditioned to deal with grief it is a wonder anyone is walking around today in any form of healthy psychological state. Some might argue that we are not. Yet, somehow we manage to make our way through and function at some level of normal. God has made us incredibly resilient.

The subject of grief work was never discussed until one doctor decided to study the taboo subject. Elizabeth Kubler-Ross and her book *On Death and Dying*, is often referred to in any book or seminar dealing with grief. Most are quick to object to her idea of stages of grief. If Kubler-Ross had meant that we go through stages, never to return to them then I would object as well. Kubler-Ross' main idea was not to codify a final theory of grief, but to start a discussion on grief. On that she succeeded very nicely. Since her groundbreaking research on grief and dying, grief counseling has become a major industry it seems.

Kubler-Ross referred to five stages of grief. We will look at those, understanding that these are not stages one works through in order, moves on and never returns. These stages, as we call them, can be experienced in any order. A person may go through two, only to find they are back at the first again. People move in and out of these stages. They often experience them in a different order. Since Kubler-Ross referred to them as stages, and I do not know of a better term to use, we will talk about the five stages of grief. Those stages are:

> Denial
> Anger
> Bargaining
> Depression
> Acceptance.

Understanding these stages, or facets of grief, helps us understand the person who is dealing with them. We shall look at each one a little closer.

Denial

Denial is often the first stage a person experiences in grief. This may be seen in a number of different ways. Initially, there may be total unbelief that the person has died. What seems to be a total refusal to accept reality is simply a defense mechanism for the brain. When the news of a loss is too much for the brain to deal with it simply refuses to accept it. While this denial is taking place, the brain, on a deeper level, is processing this latest news and trying to determine how it should respond to it.

A person experiencing denial in grief may deny the person has died. They may also talk about how this all seems to be a dream. There is the hope that at some point they will wake up and find that none of this ever happened. When I was a child, my younger brother died. I remember there were several years when I would think, "Maybe I can wake up and all of this will have been a bad dream. My brother will still be alive and we can grow up together." I never woke up to find it was a dream; I eventually stopped thinking and hoping it was a dream. Most people do not take years to reach that conclusion.

Some people have shared that even while they are planning the funeral, they keep expecting to see their loved one walk in the door. On one level they understand that this person is dead and they are trying to deal with it. On another level, they are still in denial, expecting to find very soon that it is not true.

It is not uncommon for people to say they feel the presence of the deceased at some point after the death. For some this is a comforting thought. I try not to take away any comfort a person has, as long as it is not causing harm. While some suggest that feeling the presence of the deceased is the dead attempting to contact the living; others, I think more correctly, have compared it to the phantom-limb syndrome.

When a person loses an arm or a leg, for some time after that, they report feeling pain or itching in the missing limb. This occurs because it takes some time for the body and the mind to adjust to not having that limb. These feelings of the presence of the deceased may well be the mind attempting to adjust to not having the loved one with them any more.[1]

Anger

As a grieving person works through the denial of grief, they will come to understand that this did in fact happen. As they realize the reality of their loss you can expect to see anger. An interesting aspect of anger is that a person cannot simply be angry. They must be angry at something or someone. The anger the bereaved feels must be directed toward someone or something. If you are close to the one grieving, or if you plan to be close to help them, be aware. Their anger may be directed at you. This can be unsettling. You are trying to help them, why should they be mad at you? Keep in mind that anger is a facet of grief. Anger needs a person or thing to be directed toward. If it is you, just hold on. Do not let this ruin a friendship. Recognize that the anger will pass and you will be in position to help further.

When your friend is expressing anger at you, it might be helpful to think of a scenario of an injured dog. While the dog is in pain, he will lash out and bite anyone who comes around, including his beloved owner. The dog does not understand why he hurts. He is acting to protect himself without thought to whom he is attacking. After the dog has gotten help and is no longer in pain, he will be just as loving toward his owner as he was before. When a person is experiencing grief, many times they will react without realizing why they are doing what they do. When they are in a clearer frame of mind, they will appreciate the fact that you have stayed to help.

Sometimes the object of one's anger can make someone else uncomfortable. You may know, or feel strongly that the doctors did everything possible to save the deceased, yet the bereaved is lashing out at the doctors, talking about how they failed to do what they should. Sometimes the bereaved may direct his or her anger at the person who died. "How could she leave me like this!" may be heard. Still other times the person directs their anger at God. They blame God for taking their loved one, or allowing it to happen.

I would suggest the same response to each of these expressions of anger. Keep quiet. Let the person know you are hearing them and let them rant. You might need to intervene to keep them from doing something that will cause regret later, such as making a phone call to tell the physician off. Otherwise, let them express their thoughts no matter how wrong you know them to be. Chances are the one grieving knows deep down that they are wrong. However, they are angry and they have to direct it somewhere.

While some will disagree with me here, I believe this goes for the expression of anger at God. God, more than any of the rest of us, knows what this person is going through. God made them; He knows the reaction they will have to grief. God knows what they need better than you, me or the grieving person can know. I believe that God is a big God who is able to take the anger from his creation and not get His feelings hurt from it. If you want to look at an example of this read the biblical book of Job. Job expressed anger at God for his plight. While God did come and set Job straight on who he was to even question God, still God considered Job righteous and even required Job's friends to ask Job to intervene on their behalf for God's forgiveness toward them.

Once the anger has passed, maybe several days later you might ask them about something they said. If they still feel that there was someone in the wrong you can talk about the facts then. Until that time, they are not going to hear you any way. Be quiet and be there for them.

Another way that anger may be expressed is through guilt. The bereaved may express thoughts such as, "If only I had stayed at home that day." or "If only I had listened when she said she was sick." At times there may be reason for the guilty feeling, at others it is without merit. Still, this is anger being expressed inwardly. We tend to want to fix things and tell the person that there was nothing they could do. There may not be any harm in this, but do not be surprised if your friend does not accept your reasoning right then. Let them work through their anger in a safe manner and perhaps talk about it at a later time, if you feel you must.

Bargaining

Once the anger has subsided, at least for the moment, bargaining is often the next aspect of grief. Bargaining often takes the form of making promises to God. It may be that if God will bring back the deceased, the bereaved will seek a deeper role for God. "God if you will bring back my brother, I will be a missionary." or "God if you will bring back my daddy, I will be in church every Sunday with him."

The bargaining may not be to bring the deceased back, but to take away the pain of grief. "God if you will take away this pain, I will read my Bible every day." "God, if you will ease this pain I am feeling, I will go to church every Sunday."

There is not much you can do during this stage of grief. Again, just be available to listen. If your friend decides they are going to do something in order to bring their loved one back, depending on what they are going to do, you might want to encourage them to wait. It will not hurt them to go to church, or read their Bible. But if they decide they are going to quit their job and begin preaching, you might suggest that they wait until they have dealt with this grief first. It is usually best not to make major decisions while in the midst of grief.

Depression

As the reality of the loss begins to set in and the anger subsides, the grieving person starts to realize that no amount of bargaining will change the fact that their loved one is dead. Here is where depression starts to set in. Depression is a normal part of grief, just like everything else we have looked at so far. This is not the debilitating clinical depression that requires professional help to overcome, although it can develop into that. This is a despair of not being able to cope with the loss. The grieving recognizes that they cannot change what has happened, and they do not know how to overcome the feelings they have, so they despair.

When someone is dealing with depression, they will often cut off communication from others and withdraw into themselves.[2] They simply do not want to talk to other people and they do not want to hear from others.

Some other evidences of depression are a loss of appetite and an inability to do simple chores. This can be upsetting to the bereaved because they may feel that they are losing their minds. This is not a sign of going crazy though, it is a sign of being temporarily overloaded. The mind is working with too many thoughts and feelings for the brain to handle; thus, it shuts down portions for a brief time to deal with the volume.[3]

You need to recognize that depression is part of grief. You cannot stop it. During this time you should stay in close contact with your friend. They may not want to talk. That is fine, you just need to see them and know that they are okay. You can reassure them if they start thinking they are losing their mind because they cannot remember where they put their car keys. Especially if they find they are carrying the keys around with them as they look. Let them know that this is all part of grief. The mind is trying to cope with all the information and changes it is having to process. Assure them that things will get better.

Sometimes a person's grief gets complicated. If they seem to be getting deeper and deeper into grief, help them find help to deal with it. This may be professional counseling, a grief support group, or a book about grief that will help them.

So, how do you know things are not going right? While some difficulty functioning from time to time is expected, are they simply unable to function at all? Is there an extreme focus on the death? Sure, your friend thinks about this death more than anyone else. Is that all he thinks about? As time goes on, other thoughts should become a part of life. If not, he or she may need some help. You might see extreme bitterness, anger or guilt. Again, these are normal, to a point. When it becomes extreme, something is wrong. Has your friend stopped caring about their personal hygiene? This may be an indication of clinical depression. If she begins to abuse alcohol or drugs, you need to step in and get her some help. While an occasional report of seeing the deceased, or hearing his or her voice is normal, if your friend is having these times more often, or more intense visions or hearings, seek help for them. If, over time you see your friend continue to withdraw from others or express a constant feeling of hopelessness, something is not progressing correctly in their grief. If your friend starts talking about dying or suicide, look for help right away. You must take these thoughts seriously. Let the professional determine if there is no reason to worry.

Acceptance

Finally, after going through some, or all of these stages, perhaps multiple times, the bereaved will reach acceptance. This cannot be rushed. How long it takes depends on the individual, the circumstances of the death and the relationship between the bereaved and the deceased. There is no way to put a schedule on grief. It will take as long as it takes. You, I, nor the grieving person can rush this process. It will take the time it takes.

There are some things that can hinder reaching this point though. One is the failure to take the death seriously. That applies both to the griever and to the comforter. This can actually prevent reaching the point of acceptance.[4] You need to acknowledge that the deceased is dead. You need to acknowledge that your friend is hurting. This is a very real hurt. You may not understand the pain, but know that there is pain. Many times people will offer a reminder of the deceased's eternal destiny. This is done in an attempt to comfort the one grieving. However, these words seldom help at the time. What the person grieving is actually dealing with is the personal pain death has inflicted.[5] While there are times a reminder of the eternal destiny can bring comfort, most of the time that it is offered, it does not.

We have barely touched the surface of the issue of grief. There are people who have dedicated their lives to study grief and death. They are still learning new things. So, with your limited understanding of grief, how can you actually be of comfort to someone who has lost a loved one? Whether you are a minister, a church member, family member or just a good friend, what can you do? The rest of this book will outline one plan of action to show support and offer encouragement to someone who is going through this difficult time. This is one plan. Take it; modify it as you feel the need so that it becomes your plan. The important thing is to have a plan and then work that plan.

2 INITIAL RESPONSE

We all have an idea of what a person should do to help those who are grieving, or at least we think we have an idea. We think we are supposed to tell the griever that things will be okay. We expect that we are to have just the right words to bring comfort and ease the pain our friend is experiencing. We think we need to have a verse of scripture that will help our friend through this time. After all, is that not the correct Christian response? You may have some things in your mind right now that you think you are supposed to say when you walk in the door. What I am saying is that you do not need to do any of those things; and in fact, you probably should not do any of those things. There is nothing you can say that will make the pain go away. Chances are, the only thing you can say that will be remembered beyond that moment, will be the wrong thing. Do not worry about having the right thing to say. All you really need to do is show up.

There have been numerous times when I have been called to a home because of a death. Sometimes that death was expected, sometimes it was sudden. On many of those occasions, I have shown up at the house and spoken to the ones who were grieving. I would tell them that I am sorry. I may have given a hug or put my hand on a shoulder. Sometimes I would not do any of those things.

What I say and how I provide a touch depends on the person I am with and what I think they are comfortable with. The amazing thing to me is that often, after that initial contact, I have found myself sitting or standing in a corner of the room, watching to see if there is anything I need to help with. On many occasions, I have simply been there. I did absolutely nothing. I have left that home, or hospital room feeling that I had been an absolute failure in providing comfort to this particular family. What is amazing to me is that some time later, maybe a week, two weeks or even a month later I will hear from someone else how the family has been going on and on about how much it meant to them for me to be there. They will say something about how comforting it was to see me standing there. All I did was let them know I was there and available for whatever they needed. They did not need anything, except to know that I was there. They could call on me if needed. I felt like I had done nothing, they felt like I had been a tremendous comfort, and they have used those very words.

Where most people get in trouble in the initial stage of grief ministry is trying to do something they think will help, and doing the wrong thing. Sometimes those nice sayings we always hear people repeat are not helpful. They are said because the person does not know what to say, but believes they need to say something. Often, they end up hurting those who are grieving even more. I am referring to sayings like, "God needed her voice in His choir." or "God needed him more than you did." Even if you really believe that to be true, it is not comforting to a person who has just learned that their loved one is dead. As we have mentioned earlier, reminding the grieving of the deceased's eternal destiny seldom helps, especially in the initial stages of grief. They are dealing with the personal pain the death has caused them. It is much better to walk in, express sorrow and just be there.

I have struggled at times about how to express sorrow. For me, the phrase, "I am sorry for your loss," sounds so canned. It sounds like I learned it from a police show on television. It seems false to say I am sorry for the death of a dear saint of God. After all, they are enjoying the pleasures of Heaven. Still, I am sorry for those who grieve. I understand they are experiencing pain. I am sorry for that. How you say it, I suppose is not so as important as being there to say it. Let the grieving person know that you are there, that they have your sympathy and that you will be there for them. Then stand or sit with them, step to the side if that seems best. You have no purpose after that except to be there. If you do see something that needs to be done, step up and do it.

What kind of things might need to be done? Certainly if the person breaks down crying, if there is no one else there to comfort them, you should step in. My shoulders have never gotten soggy from someone crying on them. My shirt might have, but it can be washed. Most of my life I have offered my shoulder for someone to cry on. If someone else is there to comfort them, stand by. You may be needed later. Sometimes the things you do to comfort someone may not seem comforting at the time. For instance, while you are standing nearby, if you see the trash can is overflowing, see about emptying it. You may need to ask someone where it needs to be emptied, or where to find another trash bag. When you ask, someone else may take care of it, or they may let you do it. After all, who wants to be in charge of trash? Those kinds of actions, though, may get noticed and mentioned later. You may hear, "Someone took out the trash for me. I didn't have time to get it out before everyone came in. I don't know who did it, but I sure do appreciate it." Your response should be to smile and nod. They do not have to know you did it. They know it was done. They know you were there. That is enough.

Sometimes, when you walk in, it will be obvious what needs to be done. If the kitchen sink is full of dirty dishes, you can wash them. If there is something else that needs to be done, you may suggest to someone else that the dishes need to be washed. Many times there are people at the house who want to help, but simply cannot see what needs to be done. They will appreciate a suggestion that can make them helpful to the family. Of course, depending on how close you are to the friend, you may not want to jump in and starting cleaning up. You might suggest that you can do this while they are taking care of other things. If they say, "No," then honor that.

In my area of the country, whenever a death occurs, ladies in the community and the church will prepare food to bring to the family's house. That means there will need to be a place to put that food. You may need to clear the kitchen table or counter so food can be placed there. Often people focus on food and do not think of the things needed to go with it. You may need to go buy paper towels, paper plates, cups and plastic ware. You may need to buy a bag or two of ice.

One idea is to purchase a few spiral notebooks. Place one near the phone, by the door, and at the kitchen table. Make sure you or someone is near the notebook to record who called, who stopped by to visit, who brought food.[6] The funeral home may provide a booklet for these notes, but it does not hurt to have a backup plan. During the days leading up to the funeral, your friend may not be able to think clearly about anything. That is the reason for the notebooks. Someone should be available to answer the telephone. If your friend wants to talk to the person, that is fine. If not, simply tell them that he or she is not able to come to the phone at this time. Take a message and write it down in the book. This will give them a record to remember who called and allow them to return a call when they feel they are ready, if they choose to do so. After the funeral, the books can be used by your friend to make note of anyone who visits or calls. While they will probably be able to take those calls, they may not remember them later in the day. The notebook will help with that.

You might want to check and see that the bathroom is clean and well stocked for guests. Is there plenty of toilet paper, soap, and hand towels? It would be good to ask before you take on some of these jobs. Depending on your relationship and closeness with your friend, he or she may not want you doing some things. If you do help clean up, keep what you find to yourself. It is extremely bad taste to clean up for someone grieving and then tell the community what a messy housekeeper they are.

All of the work that needs to be done is not inside. It is not all cleaning and food-related. Men, look around. Does the yard need to be mowed? Is there a loose rail on the steps that you could repair, or get repaired? Look for things that need to be done. You can do them, or ask someone else to do them. But for a close friend, the most important thing to do is to be there. Be available. If your friend asks for something, be there to either provide it, or explain to them why that is not possible at this time. Let them know you care for them. Let them know you are there for them. You do not need to say anything. Sometimes all you will do is show up and that will be more help than you can imagine.

3 THE FUNERAL

If you are a minister, chances are you know what you are supposed to be doing at the funeral. If not, there are several good books on what to do, or you may need to talk to another minister who has more experience. I would suggest that anyway. They can tell you the local customs that cannot be covered in a book. For the rest of you, what are you supposed to be doing?

Some of you may have the opportunity to help with the planning of the funeral. This may be sitting at the house and talking about what your friend wants done. You may suggest some songs, who to ask to be pall bearers, or who brings the message. There may be a few who are close enough friends that you can go with the family to the funeral home. You can give input as to which casket to choose, the vault, what other services the funeral home should provide. This is not something just any friend can do. The arranging of the funeral is a very personal business transaction. I personally think it is best for everyone to pre-plan their funeral. If nothing else, have your desires written out on paper at home. For those who do not have things pre-planned, I think it is best to have someone whom you can trust to help with the decisions. Grief hampers the brain's ability to make rational decisions. This is not the time to be making major decisions and yet that is exactly what a family is expected to do at the funeral home if there is no plan. Having someone who is capable of making rational decisions there can be a tremendous help. However, you as a friend cannot insist this is best for the family. They must see the need and invite you to go with them. You can certainly offer, but if they say no, do not push the issue. If they agree to you being there, remember, you are there to give advice, not make the decisions for them. Do not lose track of your role and become too pushy. If you are a close friend, this can be a tremendous help.

The funeral provides a time for the family to find closure. It is a time for the family, as well as friends to say goodbye. While some will disagree, the funeral should be a time to honor God. Even if the deceased was not a Christian, a minister should find a way to honor God, while providing a comfort to the family.

By attending the funeral, people tell the family that they have support. The family will recognize that there are people from extended family present. They may see church members who are there for support. People from work are a welcomed sight. To know that co-workers are there to support you in this difficult time brings a comfort. Friends and neighbors are also a welcomed sight. There is nothing anyone can do at the funeral. Your presence is all that is required or expected. This is not the time to share long stories about the deceased, especially if there is a long line of people waiting to speak to the family and view the deceased. There will be plenty of people around to offer comfort if grief overwhelms the griever. You will not have to be concerned with that. You simply want to be there to show that you are supporting them, that they can count on you.

In some parts of the country, it is customary for people to go from the cemetery to the home of the bereaved after the service. This is usually extended family and close friends. Since the news of the death hit the community people have been bringing food to the home. There are a lot of people coming to the house. These people are not grieving to the point that they are not eating. They want to eat. The food brought to the house needs to be set on the table or counter. Some of it may need to be warmed. If no one has thought about it already, there will need to be paper towels, paper plates, cups, plastic ware and ice. You may be able to help with this. Someone may need to set out folding chairs so people can sit down. I have known of people who stayed at the house during the funeral to make sure everything was ready when people started coming in. At times they have even cleaned the house if need be. Again, this is a job for a special friend. Would you want a stranger coming in to clean your house? Ask if it will be okay for you to clean. Try not to disturb the things that belonged to the deceased. Your friend will want to take care of that later. Simply moving it to another room may be too emotional for your friend. Sometimes, you will have to move some things. You must be very sensitive in this area.

Having someone at the house during the funeral provides another benefit. Unfortunately, we live in a world where some people stoop mighty low to take what they want. There are accounts of burglars who read the funeral announcements and steal the valuables from the house while the family and neighbors are at the church or funeral home. With someone staying at the house, you foil their plans and provide a comfort for the family that no one will know about.. By being at the house during the funeral, you will prevent the family from experiencing another loss that day. They will not lose their belongings.

Hopefully you or someone has taken care of the things mentioned in the previous chapter. If so, there will not be a lot to be done at the house at the time of the funeral. If you are wondering what you can do to help, let me suggest an e-book for you. *A Friend in Grief: Simple Ways to Help* by Ginny Callaway has a number of lists that you may find useful when looking for ways to help your friend.

There may not be a lot that you need to do because there are so many people around on the day of the funeral. If you feel you need to give up a little time for your own needs, this might be the best time to do that. Your services will be more important in the days and weeks after the funeral.

4 DEVELOPING A PLAN

After the funeral is over, for many, the need to offer comfort is over. As a society we are conditioned to believe grief needs to be dealt with quickly and move on. The idea is suggested, if not stated, that three weeks is plenty of time to grieve. Stop wallowing in it and buck up. Our jobs may only give us three days. We expect everyone to be over their grief in a very short time. That is simply not the case though. Grief takes a long time. If you are going to help someone through their grief, you need to be committed to the long haul.

I have served for a number of years as a pastor. I have also talked with a number of pastors over the years. I have discovered, we really do not do a good job of ministering to the grieving after the funeral. Ministers are usually good at being there in the initial stage, but we just do not continue for the long haul. That was the reason I started writing this book in the beginning. Then I realized that ministers might not be the only ones who need, or want to know how to help those grieving over the long haul. For pastors, in our defense, we want to help. We intend to make some visits later on. The problem is that living keeps getting in the way. Sermon preparation, hospital emergencies, committee meetings, denominational concerns, not to mention our own family issues, crowd out the time to make that bereavement visit. In other words, pastors do not follow-up because they do not have a plan, or else, do not know how to work their plan. Anyone else who wants to help a friend in grief will need a plan, or else life will get in your way as well.

So, what kind of plan do you need? I will not be so arrogant as to suggest I have the only real plan. I will not tell you that this is the best plan.

What I will do is lay out _a_ plan. You may have another plan, you might find a way to tweak this plan and make it better. The important thing at this point is that you have a plan. Create a schedule and then keep to your schedule. It will have to be flexible, but you cannot let it bend too much so that it becomes ineffective.

So, what is the plan? You know your friend best. What do they seem to need the most right now? You might need to visit daily with them. You might want to call them once a week and check on them. You will have to decide what your friend's needs are and how to meet them.

In addition to what you see as a need, let me offer this plan for the long term. You might see more you need to do, or you may feel there is less you should do to help your friend. The idea is based on what I have seen different hospice organizations use in their bereavement program. The plan calls for contact with the grieving person on a regular, prescribed schedule. I have looked at different ways of contact. I have tried phone calls, visits and letters. I have gotten the most response from the letters I have sent. Of course, there is a combination that would work best.

You may want to adjust this plan to better fit your style and the situation. Start out with a phone call each month. Just to let the grieving friend know that you are thinking about them. The call does not have to be long, or it could be several hours. That really depends on you and your friend. Along with the phone call, an occasional visit is good. You might arrange this during your phone call. If they express a need to talk, if they sound more "down" than usual, plan to make a visit. The other part of the plan is to send letters.

Writing letters is becoming a lost art. Why should I write a letter when I can pick up the phone and call? Have you ever gotten a phone call that you wanted to hear again? Unless you record your calls you do not have that call to listen to again. Of course messages can be sent by email and social media. You could send a text. Still, the ability to sit in a chair and hold a piece of paper in your hand as you read the words, again, is special. The fact that someone took the time to write that letter makes it even more special. That may sound like you are going to have to invest in a nice pen and stationary. I admit, I am falling in love with the art of writing. I have more pens than I do stationary, but that is not necessary. Even if you type your letter on the computer and print it, this will still be a tremendous blessing to the person receiving the letter. At least that is what people have told me after they received one of my letters. As a pastor and a chaplain, I have sent form letters to people who were grieving. I try to personalize the letter in some way, but they all say about the same thing. I have heard, both directly and indirectly, that these letters were a wonderful prize. One lady told me, a year later, that she still has every letter I sent her. So how many letters do you write? I would suggest four letters over the course of a year. The timing for the letters is, two months after the death, six months after the death, nine months after the death and one year after the death.

A letter two months after the death will be coming around the time that the grieving friend realizes that everyone has left and they are on their own. At six months, many bereaved report that they thought they had finally turned the corner and were doing okay with the death. Then, all of sudden, it comes back full force on them again. Nine months seems to be another time where the bereaved feels they are slipping back into the darkness of grief. Of course, the one year anniversary of a death is usually hard for those who grieve. It brings back all the feelings and fears again. To have something in their hands that reminds them that you are still with them and that you understand something of what they are dealing with can be a tremendous blessing for those who grieve.

This is part of the plan. I would suggest that you also plan to do some remembrance for the deceased and help the bereaved plan for the holidays. We will look more at these parts later in the book. Keep in mind that grieving is often more difficult on a special date, such as the deceased's birthday, or some other special day. If the deceased was a spouse, then the wedding anniversary may be a difficult time. Keep these dates in mind. You might want to make an extra phone call, a visit, or send an extra letter on those days.

This plan works through the first year of grief. That is not to suggest that your friend will be over their grief in a year. Some people say they had moved on by that time, others have reported that it took longer. Two years is a time-frame that is often talked about. The first year is a year of firsts. This will be the first time your friend experiences the birthday of the deceased without him or her. It will be the first time your friend goes through the holidays without their loved one. If your friend is doing well at the end of the first year, you can relax your support. Keep in contact and be there if they seem to fall back. If they are not doing well at the end of the year, that is okay. There is nothing wrong with them and they need to hear you tell them that. Plan to stay in touch. Make the phone calls, visit, and perhaps send some more letters. These may be more of a friendly letter specific to the relationship you have with your friend. Your friend is the only one who can say when they are through their grief.

This is _a_ plan to help a friend through their grief. If you read this and think, "I can do better;" go for it. If your plan works better, let me know, or write about it yourself. Let people know how we can help those who grieve.

5 THE SCHEDULE

So, you have a plan. You really want to be there to help your friend. You know when you want to make the phone calls, you know when you want to send the letters. How do you keep up with it? That is an entire year you have to remember to do these things.

The first idea is to write it on your calendar. This might be a paper calendar on the wall at home, or it may be the calendar on your computer, or on your phone. You will write each month when you make that telephone call, depending on the frequency of your calls. If you have scheduled a monthly call and then in the middle of the month feel you need to make an extra call, pick up the phone and call. The schedule is to help you, not limit you. You want to make sure you call at least that often, if you feel the need to call more at some time, pick up the phone and call.

On that same calendar, write in the dates you want to make a visit. Again, if you call and feel you need to make a visit, then do so. These are the visits you do not want to forget about because you got busy. You would then write in each date you want to send the letter. Count from the day-of-death two months, six months, nine months and one year. The letter does not have to be sent, or received exactly on that date. Sending it that month will be okay. I like to send it close to the date. By that I mean, if the date-of-death was near the first of the month, I try to send the letter around the first of the month. If the death was near the end of the month, I will send the letter near the end of the month. While working with hospice, I would try to send all the letters around the first of the month, because I had so much more to do the rest of the month. As long as the letter gets to your grieving friend on or around that month they will appreciate it.

When you are putting things on an electronic calendar, you have helpful tools, such as typing in an appointment and have that reoccur. Determine how often that reoccurs and how long it will reoccur. If you have a smart phone, there is probably an app that will take care of scheduling this for you. If there is not one now, there will probably be one very soon. Many probably know of some even higher tech system to keep up with all of this. What about those of us who are low tech? You may not have a smart phone. You may not be that comfortable with a computer. Maybe your paper calendar has so much on it you are afraid you will miss a letter during the year. What can you do?

Another idea that I have seen in practice for scheduling was used in the military. There may be another name for it, but what I have heard is a "Tickler File." This is my suggestion for setting up this tickler file. Take an index card file box like a recipe box. Place dividers in the box for each month. Take an index card and write your friend's name at the top of the card along with his or her address and telephone number. Put the name of the person who died on the card and the date of death. You might want to put the relationship of the deceased to the griever if you think you might not remember in a year. If you know it, write the deceased's date of birth, so you can remember to make an extra check during that time. Then, on the card you will put the dates for each letter and each visit you are planning. If you are planning a phone call each month, there is no need to put that on the card. You will also want to put a reminder to yourself about the Remembrance and Grief in the Holidays. Again, we will talk about these later in the book, but put a reminder here for you.

Each month you will look behind the tab for that month. Take out the card and see what needs to be done. Put that card where you will see it and be reminded of the action to be taken. Once you have completed everything for that month – telephone call, letter, visit, etc. – put the card behind the tab for the next month. Thus, each month you are reminded by the card of what needs to be done and can take care of it. This plan works well, if you are helping several people through their grief. Seldom does death come only once a year.

Ministers may find this system handy also. Behind each monthly tab there are multiple cards. If there is no date on the card for a letter or visit, then you simply need to make a phone call, and/or plan a remembrance or grief in the holidays program. Then place the card in the next month. If there is a date for a letter, write the letter and mail it. If there is a date for a visit, plan that visit. This will ensure you make the contact you want to with your friend and they do not get pushed aside because of other pressing issues.

Is it really necessary to do all of this? In some cases, it probably is not. If you see your friend every day at work, or every week at church, you may not need to make a phone call every month. Your phone calls will be more to follow-up if they seem to be having a bad day when you see them. I believe the letters are an important part of the plan. You may feel, however, that you will not have to write as many letters. As I said earlier, adjust the plan so that it fits you and your friend the best. Keep in mind that you are trying to meet your friend's needs. Do not make the schedule only about your convenience or needs.

6 THE MESSAGE

So what is the message we hope to convey with these phone calls and letters? First and foremost, the message should be, "I care and I am here for you." That may be all your friend needs, is to know that someone cares, that he or she has a safety net, someone they can turn to if grief gets to be too much for them to handle. Let them know you are praying for them. They do not have to face this journey alone. You are bringing them before God for help and you are standing ready to help in any way possible.

Your phone calls should show that message most clearly. The phone call can simply be, "Hey, I just wanted to call and see how you are doing today." Then, let them tell you how they are doing. If this is a good day, let them share all the wonderful things that have happened. If this is a bad day, listen to them as they tell you why it is such a bad day. Understand, too, that this may be a day when anger has reared its ugly head. Your friend may seem anything but a friend today. They may tell you off for any number of things you did, or did not do. They may jump on your case for something that you have no control over. Understand, this is all part of working through grief. Do not take offense at the anger. Be glad you could be there to take it. Remember, "A fool shows his annoyance at once, but a prudent man overlooks an insult." (Prov. 12:16 NIV). If you are not the one to take the explosion of anger, someone else will and they may not understand why. They may not be able to let their friendship be deeper than the hurtful words that may spew forth. This is part of helping a friend through grief. It is not always pretty. It is not always pleasant, but it is always worth it, because this is your friend.

The second month's letter should remind your friend that they are working through grief. You might mention some of the things they may be experiencing; keeping in mind not everyone experiences the same things or at the same time. Then remind them that these things are a normal part of grief. They are acting perfectly normal if they find their memory failing at times or they have trouble finding their appetite. You want to remind them that they must work through their grief. As much as they want to avoid it or bypass it, they must work through it. Any attempt to bypass grief will only create more problems. Make sure your friend knows you are available if they need you. Since memory failure is so common, you might consider including your telephone number in the letter. They should know it, but if they cannot remember at that moment, you have helped them again.

In the six month's letter, let your friend know that you are aware of how long it has been since their loved one died. This is not just a random letter you are sending. This is because it has been six months. It is a reminder that the anger, pain, fear, and depression they might have felt are a normal part of grief. You might want to remind them that everyone grieves differently. Just because they are not grieving like their brother, does not mean they are doing it wrong. Let them know that tears are okay. Women are usually more accepting of this than men. Still, there are times that a woman thinks she should not cry. With society telling her she should be over her grief, she may be ashamed to be crying still. For men and women, tears are a part of grief. Both need to let them flow. They may not come at the most appropriate time, but we need to let them flow. Remind your friend that grieving is hard work, he or she should try to get plenty of rest. You might also let them know that grief work takes time. Our culture may say get over it, but give your friend permission to take his or her time. Again, make sure your friend knows that you are there and that they can call if they need you.

The ninth month's letter is a reminder to your friend that they may still slip back into the darkness of grief. You can remind them of some things to help them cope with all they are dealing with. Offer some simple tips on dealing with grief. Earlier, these tips might not be accepted. Now they will be read and cherished. Your friend will be comforted by your thoughtfulness.

The one year letter is a notice that you have not forgotten. It says, I understand that this has been a difficult year. It lets your friend know that while you do not know "exactly how they feel," you do understand something of what they are dealing with. After all, you have walked through the grief process with them this past year. Let them know that this is not the end of their grief. There will still be good days and bad days. Hopefully the good days will be more than the bad days. Also let them know that you will still be available if they need you. I generally end my phone calls, letters and such after a year, unless I see that they need more support. You have to evaluate this yourself and decide. Even after ending the scheduled contact, you want them to know that you are still there for them. If things get overwhelming, they can call you.

7 BEING AVAILABLE

When there has been a death, many people will come by and offer their condolences. Almost as many will say, "If there is anything I can do for you let me know." If you are going to help a friend through their grief, you need to go beyond these simple acts. This is serious ministry you are carrying out. That means you have to be available if your friend needs you. That availability does not come at your convenience. It comes when your friend says, "I need someone."

I do not want to sound as if you have to give up your life in order to help your friend. There will be times that you simply cannot drop everything and go to your friend. However, you need to consider your plans and see if you do need to change them. This is to help your friend, it may also be an appointment God has made that you need to keep. When you reach out to a friend and offer to walk with them through grief, you have to be prepared for that walk to be uncomfortable and inconvenient.

There have been times that I had to cancel my entire day's schedule in order to respond to a call for help. Some of those times, as I looked back, I did not see that I had done anything that could not have been done the following day. Yet, it could not have been done later. The friend called and asked, "Can you come over?" I responded and was there. Without words, I told that friend, "I am here when you need me. I said I would be, and now you can see that it is true." There have been other times when I received a call for help. I talked with my friend for a few moments on the phone and they felt much better. They knew I was there, they felt better, and I could continue with the remainder of my schedule.

There are times your friend may ask you to help with insurance forms, or paying the bills. This can certainly be a need for someone who is dealing with grief. I have trouble dealing with insurance forms when there is nothing distracting me. I can only imagine trying to fill out forms while my mind is dealing with everything associated with grief. There may be times, though, that you sit down to help with the insurance or to help pay bills and your friend does not bring anything out to work on. When you ask, they tell you they will get it in a moment. They may start talking then. You can soon see that the insurance or the bills was simply an excuse to have you come over. Your friend may not have felt right asking you to come listen to them. They may not have even realized this is what they needed. That may well be all they needed. The next day your friend may take care of the insurance, pay the bills and do fine. That day, they needed a reason to ask you to come by so they could talk. Be grateful that they wanted you to be there. It shows a level of trust.

One lady told me that she did not want to be left alone. She wanted someone to be with her all the time. This was not because she was afraid to stay by herself, she just wanted to have someone to talk to whenever she felt like talking about her loved one. Not everyone wants or needs this kind of support. This is an example of where you have to ask what they need and then be ready to respond to the request. Few people could be available for that kind of support. Sometimes your support is not direct support. Sometimes you need to coordinate the support that is needed. If you are a man, trying to help a lady friend, or if you are a minister trying to help a church member, you certainly cannot meet these needs. You can call on others who could step in for a time. There are plenty of people who truly want to help. They just do not have a clue as to what they need to do and are not comfortable asking. When you know the need, you can tell these friends what is needed and see when someone can stay and who else you might need to ask. This is not about you providing all the care and comfort, it is about helping your friend through her grief.

After the funeral is over, your friend will have all sorts of things he or she needs to take care of. If family is not there to help, you can offer to drive your friend to take care of these errands. It will probably be safer for your friend not be driving at this point anyway. Grief is still taking up much of his or her thoughts and thus driving is not in their thoughts. Also, this is another opportunity for your friend to talk, if he or she wants to. If they simply want to sit there while you drive, that should be okay as well. Several people have told me how friends came by and helped them with thank-you cards. They may have written the cards or the family may have written the cards and the friends simply addressed them. They would do this until the family felt they could not continue. They put everything away and left the rest for another day. This is another example of how you can show someone you care by doing simple things.

You may want to suggest some activity for your friend, sometime after the funeral. Do not insist on anything, but offer suggestions. Allow your friend to cancel at the last minute if she feels she cannot go through with the activity. The activities can be a simple as taking a walk around the park. You might suggest dinner or a movie. If there is a support group that you think would be helpful to your friend, offer to go with him.

You need to be available whenever your friend needs you. Sometimes the call may come in the middle of the night. It is hard to crawl out of bed when you are sleeping soundly and you know you have a tough day ahead of you at work. If your friend calls, you need to be on your way to them. That is what being available is all about. That is what it means to walk with someone through their grief. You are there when they need you. If you want to do something on your schedule and not be inconvenienced, then find what that might be. If you say that you are there whenever you are needed, then be truthful and be there when your friend needs you.

One thing to keep in mind is that grief is not something your friend will "get over." Those who have gone through grief will tell you, they do not want to "get over it." They do not want to forget about their loved one. A person who goes through grief will also not "get back to normal." At least not in the sense others will think of getting back to normal. A person going through grief is actually working to find a new normal. They will become normal at some point. It will be a different normal from what they were before. They must learn to live with their grief. They must learn to live with a part of their lives missing from now on. In time, they will learn to live with that grief, with that loss. They will begin to function as a normal person again. They will not be the same person though. You need to keep this in mind. You may need to remind your friend at times. You might even have the opportunity to explain this to some of your other friends to prevent hurt and misunderstanding later.

8 REMEMBER

There is a lesson here that I already knew, yet, I had to relearn the hard way. I hope you can learn this lesson and not make the mistake I made. I have served for several years as a chaplain for law enforcement. Law enforcement officers have a special place in my heart. Once I heard of a deputy in a department I had served with in the past who was killed in a motor vehicle accident. I did not know the deputy, but I did know the sheriff. I called to offer my condolences to the sheriff. He was not in the office when I called and I was talking with his secretary. I explained to her that I was calling to offer my condolences for the death of the deputy. (I had momentarily drawn a blank on what the deputy's name was.) The secretary responded, "Yes, BRANDON was a special person." She really emphasized the name "Brandon." I knew immediately what was wrong. I had failed to remember this deputy, whom the secretary considered as part of her family. By not calling his name, in her mind, I had made his life trivial. That was not my intention, but that is how she perceived it. I have made it a point to never make that mistake again.

It is important that you call the deceased by name. If you are talking about your friend's mother or dad, you might be able to call them Mom or Dad, however they usually refer to them around others. It is still a good idea to refer to them by their name. This tells those around you that this person was important to you. We remember the names of those who are important to us. People who are not important, we do not bother with their names. When you call the deceased by name, you tell the one who is grieving that that person was important to you. You tell other people this person was an important person to you. That provides some comfort to those who are grieving, to know that others see their loved one as important.

One of the reasons for your telephone calls and letters is to tell the bereaved that their loved one is being remembered. Yes, you are trying to offer words of comfort to your friend who is grieving, but you often do so by letting them know that their loved one has not been forgotten. While it seems that the rest of the world has forgotten the deceased after a couple of weeks, you are saying, "I still remember them." That provides a tremendous comfort to someone who is grieving.

It is a good idea to plan something special as a remembrance for the deceased. For pastors, once a year you could plan a special time in the worship service to remember those who have died during the past year. I usually try to do this in December. Some other time might work better. I have not found that the entire service needs to be focused on remembrance. You might just take a few minutes at the beginning or the end of the service and reverently call out the names of each person who had died. After each name has been called, pray for the families and friends who remember those people, that God will provide continued comfort. You can make this as simple, or as elaborate as you want. The fact that you are willing to take time to remember those loved ones will mean a lot. Some pastors may feel it is better to plan a special time separate from the worship service. You can plan times of scripture reading, prayer, maybe a poem and a message about the importance of remembering our loved ones.

For those who are not ministers, you still can do something special for a remembrance. You might want to plan a remembrance service if there are several friends you are helping. You could plan a small gathering at yours or your friend's house to invite family and friends to remember the deceased. You might want to allow time for people to share a brief story they remember from the life of the deceased.

You can plan for a time of remembrance even if it is just you and your friend. If you have some pictures bring them out and reminisce with your friend over those pictures. You might just take some time and share some stories about the deceased. You could ask your friend to bring out some pictures for you to look at. As you look at the pictures, ask your friend about any stories he or she recalls. You encourage that and listen with interest. Just getting a few people together to share their memories will be a time your friend will cherish. You will be surprised at how much the simple act of remembering will mean to a person who is working through grief.

When planning a time of remembrance, do not plan it too soon after the death. The anniversary of the death might not be a good time, but somewhere around a year after the death should be good. This gives the grieving friend time to adjust and be able to enjoy the time without falling to pieces with sorrow. If your friend does begin to cry and seem overwhelmed emotionally, allow her to express her sorrow. You might need to cancel, or postpone the rest of the time, or your friend may want you to continue once she has had a good cry. Let your friend guide you in what to do.

9 HOLIDAYS

Grief is difficult to work through any time. For many, it is especially difficult during the holidays. We tend to think of Thanksgiving and Christmas as times for family to get together. Everything you see and hear about these holidays suggests family, laughter and good times together. When a member of the family is not present the pain can be intensified. It is important to recognize this and look for ways to provide extra support during the holidays.

One obvious idea to help someone during this time might be to invite them to spend the holidays with you and your family. But, suppose your friend has family coming over, or they are meeting family somewhere? There is still the pain of knowing that ONE person will not be there this year. How can you help with this?

Despite the busyness normally experienced during the holidays, you might need to plan some extra time to spend with your friend. They may need a little extra attention to help them cope with this unexpected pain. Again, just being there may be enough. You might need to be a listening ear or simply give your friend permission to do something different this year. Many people have reported that they could not bear to carry out the same holiday traditions without their loved one. Some people need to know that it is alright to do some things differently. I talked with a lady one time who was overwhelmed with the idea of decorating her house for Christmas – a time she and her husband always enjoyed together. This year her husband was not there to help her decorate. After talking with her about her husband and what they used to do to decorate, she asked me if I thought it would be wrong to not put any decorations up this year. I assured her I did not think God would be angry with her for not decorating the house for

Christmas. We talked about how her grown children might feel about the lack of decorations. I told her that it was really up to her. If she wanted to decorate the house, she should. If she felt she could not handle it emotionally, then there was no reason she should have to decorate. She sounded so relieved when we got off the phone. I have no idea what she decided to do with the decorations. Whatever she did, she knew it was her decision. She was not doing this because she had to.

There are a number of other things that you can do for someone who is working through grief during the holidays. Let me suggest a resource that will cover most of those ideas and will be fairly simple for you as well. If your friend's loved one was a hospice patient, chances are he or she will receive an invitation to attend a meeting about grief and the holidays. If that is the case, then encourage your friend to go to this meeting. You might even offer to go with your friend. If your friend's loved one was not a hospice patient, then check with your local hospice about their grief and the holidays meeting. As far as I know, every hospice will have this kind of meeting. Usually it will be sometime from late September to early November. Make sure that the meeting is open to the public, and then encourage your friend to attend this meeting. In this meeting, someone with training in grief work will share some of the issues the bereaved might experience. They will also talk about some ways to cope with the holidays.

Just knowing what to expect can be a tremendous help to someone who is grieving. To learn some coping mechanisms is great. To have someone give permission to change or bypass certain traditions can be freeing to the one who is experiencing grief. Offer to go with your friend to this meeting. They may be reluctant to go alone. Once your friend gets there he or she may find that knowing there are others who feel the same way they do is a freeing piece of information.

For the friend who wants to keep their traditions, or at least part of their traditions, encourage them to plan early for the holidays. When shopping lists are made, your friend can shop when he or she feels strong. When those days come when your friend does not feel like doing anything it will be okay. You can help your friend with the planning, determine what needs to be done, what shopping needs to be done and what priority needs to be set for each thing. You might offer to help with some of the tasks your friend needs to get done. If she does not feel like shopping, ask if you can do the shopping with the list that has already been made.

Keep in mind that Thanksgiving and Christmas are not the only holidays your friend will be dealing with. If your friend's father died, the next Father's day may be hard for him to face. The birthday of the deceased will be difficult as well. Take note of when these events take place. Mark them on your calendar and be prepared. You might want to make an extra telephone call. A card around that time might be helpful. Knowing that this special date is approaching, you can be observant to see if your friend needs some additional attention.

10 SPECIAL CIRCUMSTANCES

You need to remember that no two people grieve the same. Also, there is no grief that is harder than another. Still, there are certain types of grief that often have a similar element for some people. You should be aware of these elements and consider how to respond to them. At the same time, do not be concerned if you do not see your friend responding to that element. That may not be an issue for them, or at least not at the moment.

The first type of grief to consider is the death of an infant – a newborn, a stillbirth, or a miscarriage. The loss of an infant has a lonely dimension to it. The mother is the only one who really knows the child.[7] However, do not forget the father. While he has not become acquainted with the infant to the degree of the mother, still he is experiencing a sense of loss. Too often in a miscarriage or stillbirth, people focus on the mother and forget that the father may be grieving as well. One of the difficult things with this type of grief is that the parents' grief is intensified by the need to explain the significance of a child no one else knows.[8]

So, how can you help? First, remember the father in the grief process. Be sure to ask about him, how he is doing, and maybe check on him yourself. If you are a man and your friend is a father whose wife had a miscarriage, consider working through these steps with him just as you would if it was one of his parents who had died. Another thing you can do when the deceased is an infant is to listen to the parents. For you, it may not seem like there is much to talk about. For the parents it is important to know that others realize this child was a person. This was not a mass of cells with no meaning in life. This was their son or their daughter. Let them tell you how this baby responded in the womb to different things. Let them tell you the sense of connection they had with this child. Let them see you are anxious to hear what you lost by never having been able to meet this child. You will provide comfort to the parents and you will just possibly recognize that you too have experienced a loss. You may find that this was indeed a special human being whose life was cut off way too soon.

A number of young women who have undergone an abortion report some of the same feelings as the parents of a stillborn baby. They may not feel free to express their grief however, since they made the choice to end the pregnancy. Still they may be grieving. If you know a woman who had an abortion, reach out to her and be willing to listen to her. You may be the only one who is willing to try to understand. This is not the time to talk about what was right or wrong about the decision. This is a time to help someone who may be grieving, but does not feel she is allowed to express that grief.

The death of a child often focuses on the mother. The father may not show his grief in a way we expect. I have known men who would work all day long on their job, or some other physical work. To look at them you would think nothing had happened. If you know the person well, you would know that they are hurting. They are experiencing grief. This is the only way they feel comfortable expressing it. Because they express it this way, many people do not realize these men are grieving and therefore do not offer any words of comfort or concern. We need to change our perception. Also realize that if there are siblings in the home, they too will be grieving. Children grieve differently, still, they grieve. Recognize that and take some time with them as well. In the death of a child, there is a search for significance. The parents want to make sure the child is not forgotten.[9] While it is important to call the deceased by name, when the deceased is a child, this is especially important. Simply calling the child by name will provide so much comfort to the parents. It lets them know that their son or daughter has not been forgotten. They are still remembered by those outside of the family. As you listen to your friend tell about this child, share any experiences or thoughts you have about the child. There may be a story you remember about his child that will show the parents that you too see the significance of this child, and that you have memories that will not soon fade away.

Another special case to consider is suicide. Suicide has been described as having a shattered dimension. Most times, suicide leaves a lot of unanswered questions. There is a lot of self-questioning as to what I could have done to prevent this tragedy. Was there a sign here, did they suggest their intentions there? Before a family can really begin to grieve after a suicide they must piece the events together and understand, to some degree, what happened. This grief is often accompanied with an intense sense of guilt. People look back and see all sorts of signs that this was coming. Even if there was no way to see it, people will see things in retrospect that they will convince themselves they should have recognized and taken action to stop the suicide. So they grieve and they feel guilty at the same time. While you can remind your friend that they could not have known what the deceased was going to do, do not try to convince them of that. You may point it out, but if they want to argue the point, let it go. Perhaps when they are able to think through all of this more logically, they will be able to see what you are saying.

For now, simply let them know that you are there with them. You are not passing judgment. You do not blame them and it is your opinion that they should not blame themselves either. Then leave it alone and be the friend that you are.

What about those who grieve after a long illness? There are times that you may not see any signs of grief. Your friend may seem, almost relieved. Many people see this and either think your friend is really strong, or else they may think your friend did not properly love the deceased. When a person has been caring for a loved one with an extended illness there may well be a sense of relief. This is not an indication of a lack of love. It is the reality that this illness has taken a lot of your friend's time and life. Now there is the chance to get back to a sense of normalcy. You need to understand too that with a long illness, there has been a certain amount of grieving taking place during the illness. Professionals refer to this as anticipatory grief. It is grief in anticipation of the death that is sure to come in a relatively short time. That does not mean that there is no grief when the loved one dies. It simply means that some of the intensity of the grief has already played out in your friend's emotions. There will still be the feelings of grief. Your friend will still experience the stages of grief. They may not be as intense. Others may not recognize them. You will be able to see them, because you are aware of what is happening and you are looking for those signs. Keep in touch with your friend. Let them express their grief when they are ready. Let them know they should not feel guilty if they do not break down in tears every time their loved one's name is mentioned. Remind them that they have already experienced a great deal of grief, even before the death and their response now, is acceptable.

When considering those with long illnesses, do not forget those who are taking care of someone with dementia. Alzheimer's is becoming more common it would seem. For the friend whose loved one is facing this, grief is being expressed before the death. Many who have a loved one dealing with any form of dementia express that they lost their loved one long before they died. The friend may be taking care of their parent or spouse and have that person not know who they are. It is hard to take care of Mama when Mama does not know who you are. A person dealing with a dementia patient requires a lot of patience. As that person becomes more of a stranger to the caregiver, it may become harder to be patient with them. When the caregiver loses patience, there can be a sense of guilt. When the person dies, there really is a sense of relief. This causes a sense of guilt because your friend may not have been so nice at times to their loved one. They may feel their loved one died years ago, their body stayed on and someone else occupied that body. Your friend will still need your support. He or she will still experience grief, it will just present itself in a different way.

11 SELF CARE

As a hospice chaplain, one of the things I found myself doing more than I expected was telling caregivers they needed to take care of themselves. We can become so focused on helping someone else that before long we have let ourselves run down. The problem, then, is that you cannot help someone else when you are sick or exhausted. If you want to take care of others, you must take care of yourself.

The first caution I would offer is to not take on too much in the way of grief ministry. There is a limit to how many people you can help through grief. A small hospice may provide bereavement support to a hundred people at any given time. Most of this support will be a phone call here and a letter there. Most of those bereaved will have a support system so that the hospice person does not have to get too involved. Support is offered through monthly support meetings. If the hospice person finds that they need to become more involved then they know to be aware of how much their support is draining from them. Even a well trained hospice bereavement specialist can only provide in-depth support to a limited number of people. You have most likely not received the training, nor do you have the resources to support a large number of friends at any given time.

So how many people should you be walking with through grief? That is a question I cannot answer. You will need to consider how much you are emotionally tied to these friends. How much time are they taking? How much are they draining you physically, emotionally and spiritually? All of this has to be taken into account when you determine how much you can do. Most people I know are not really able to tell when they are taking on too much. That would include me. There are times when my wife will tell me, "Don't you think you need to take a break?" or "I think you need to back off and take some time for you." Then, I realize that I have taken on too much. I need to try not to take on any more people whom I can help. I am not helping them if I am tearing myself down. There is no magical number, you have to see what each person is doing to you and how you are handling it.

I can hear the pastors say, "I have a lot of church members who are going through grief. I can't leave them without help. I will have to keep pushing on." Pastor, you are not exempt from needing to take care of yourself. I know that some churches expect their pastor to be some super high holy man who can do all things. Maybe they have gotten that idea because we have promoted it as pastors. The truth is, you are limited to what you can do just like everyone else. If you are finding a large number of bereaved in your church, maybe you need to involve the deacons, elders or some other group within your church. Since pastors are called to equip the saints (Eph. 4:12), maybe you would do well to equip some in your church who can take on some of the grief ministry within your church. Then you will be able to focus your time on "prayer and the ministry of the Word." (Acts 6:4).

For others, if you find you are quite busy helping people through grief, maybe you can enlist some help as well. You might want to get some people in your church involved. Maybe there is a group at work, or in another group you are a part of. You can train them what you have learned, show them where they can get other resources they might need and get them involved. Chances are they will share some of the same friends you have. If someone else is walking with them, you can simply call from time to time and let them know you are thinking of them. You are freed up to focus on the others you are walking with through grief.

Make sure you plan time to rest. While you might have to get out of bed some nights to go to a friend who needs you, most nights you should be able to get the sleep you need. Plan for it. You also need to plan for some time when you can get away from the pressure of helping others and just relax yourself. You might need to plan a vacation. There might be times you need to stay at home and turn off the phone. I know that is a shocking thought, but if you cannot get any downtime otherwise, then it needs to be done. You have got to be able to recharge your batteries. I would suggest that you attend, and stay involved in a local church. Your spiritual battery will run down quickly doing this kind of ministry. You need to have it charged on a regular basis. Make some time to read a good book, nothing on grief. You have plenty of chances to read those. Find something else you like to read. Whether it is fiction, history, how to, whatever you find enjoyable, take time to read, to get away from the grief work you are involved in.

Look for ways to take care of yourself. Helping someone through an emotional journey like this will have an effect on you. If you do not take care of yourself, you will burn out and be of no use to anyone. A good source for ideas on taking care of yourself is Sara Anderson's ebook, *Journey With the Grieving*. This book talks about how to help someone through grief, but all through the book Sara shares ideas about how to take care of yourself. Find ideas in Sara's book or another resource, but find the ideas and use them. If not for you, do it for your friend.

APPENDIX I TWO MONTH LETTER

Dear _____,

The first few months after the death of a loved one are usually extremely difficult. I am sending you this letter to remind you that I am here to assist in any way that I can during your time of grief.

There are a variety of feelings and emotions that one experiences during the first few months following a significant loss. Some say that their memory seems to fail them, plus they experience problems eating and/or sleeping. You may have experienced some of these emotional and physical problems and possibly many more since the loss of _____.

Please know this… all of these things are normal when dealing with grief. You may be tempted to shut down emotionally and avoid grief. Just remember that you must go through your grief, you cannot go around it. Choosing to put it off or denying your grief can cause many problems in the future.

If there is anything I can to do assist you please give me a call. Also know that I am praying for you and your family.

Sincerely,

APPENDIX II SIX MONTH LETTER

Dear _____,

Regardless of how unbelievable it may seem six months have passed since the death of _____. You may have experienced pain, fear, anger, and depression among many other emotions. You have most likely discovered that recovering from the loss of a loved one takes a lot of time, effort and energy.

I simply want to reiterate a few things that you probably already know about the grief process:

1. Everyone grieves differently, in their own way and at their own pace.
2. Tears are a natural part of the process. It often seems that they come at the most inappropriate times in the most inappropriate places. But, allow them to come out. Holding tears back will result in a lot of bottled up feelings.
3. Take care of yourself. You are putting a lot of energy into grief work. Make sure you are eating and sleeping enough.
4. Be patient with yourself. The grieving process takes time.

Please call me if I can help in any way.

Sincerely,

APPENDIX III NINE MONTH LETTER

Dear _____,

I know you're going through a difficult time right now. I also know that grief can be a painful experience. Consider what one expert in grief has to say.

Alan D. Wolfelt, Ph.D. said, "My experience has taught me that we as human beings are forever changed by the death of someone in our lives. To talk about 'resolving' our own or other's grief, doesn't allow for the growth or transformation I have both experienced in myself and observed in others. Mourning is not an end, but a beginning."

There are four goals of grief work:

1. To move from numbness to successful restructuring.
2. To honor the place of what has been lost.
3. To create new patterns of action independent of the loss
4. To link hope with action.

It is normal to go through doubts about ourselves, and our faith. Normally, these are companions of grief and mourning.

Through our spiritual journey we are given three questions to tackle. Once these three questions are answered, we will not only be successful on our journey but will achieve a new vision and hope. What has changed? What is still possible in my life? How do I get there?

Finding the correct answer to these questions will help you be successful in your journey.

I am here to help in any way I can. Please feel free to call me.

Sincerely,

APPENDIX IV ONE YEAR LETTER

Dear _____,

This month marks the one-year anniversary of the death of _____. I feel sure that this year has felt like a roller coaster of emotions for you. You might still have very difficult days. Hopefully those days are fewer and do not occur as often as they once did.

As the time passes one of my hopes for you is that the memories of _____ will continue to bring you comfort and peace. *Remember that life may end, but...memories last forever.*

I will continue be here to assist you in any way that I can. Please feel free to contact me if I can help you in any way.

Sincerely,

ENDNOTES

[1] Dodd, Robert V., *When They All Go Home: What to do After the Funeral*, (1989: Nashville: Abingdon Press), 6.

[2] Ibid, 8.

[3] Manning, Doug, *Will I Survive This Pain?*, *Continuing Care Series*, Book 1, (1991: Herford, TX, In-Sight Books), 20.

[4] Dodd, 9.

[5] Ibid.

[6] Callaway, Ginny, *A Friend in Grief: Simple Ways to Help*, (2011: Fairview, NC, High Windy Press).

[7] Manning, 12.

[8] Ibid.

[9] Ibid.

RESOURCES

A Friend in Grief: Simple Ways to Help by Ginny Callaway
Fairview, NC High Windy Press

A Journey With the Grieving by Sara Anderson
Orlando, FL, Smashwords

How to Go On Living When Someone You Love Dies by Therese A. Rando PhD
Lexington, MA, Lexington Press

ABOUT THE AUTHOR

Lee Joyner has served as a pastor for over fifteen years. He has been a hospice chaplain for over five years and a law enforcement chaplain during much of that time. He has a Master of Divinity degree with a concentration in Counseling from Southeastern Baptist Theological Seminary in Wake Forest, North Carolina. Lee has had experience working with the grieving, from the earth shattering news, to the long expected and all points in between. He has helped friends and strangers deal with grief.